# Introduction to The Feeling Alphabet

i

# Introduction to The Feeling Alphabet

We work in different disciplines: psychology and education, respectively. We work with some overlapping groups and some different groups and organizations. One of us spends lots of time working in and with schools and colleges; another of us spends lots of time working in and with communities and community organizations across the globe. Together, we share a deep concern about the wellbeing of all of our children, parents, students, clients, teachers, and caring professionals. This Feeling Alphabet Activity Set is designed for all of those with whom we work worldwide.

A few words about the title of this work, which informs its meaning and use. We have deliberately used the term "The Feeling Alphabet Activity **Set**" as opposed to possible other titles such as "The Feeling Alphabet Activity **Book**" or "The Feeling Alphabet Activity **Workbook**" or just "The Feeling Alphabet." This is because we recognize that what follows is not a book, either in terms of length or depth. It is not a workbook either; the latter suggests one-off activities that may not be linked with the goal of animating a text. And the word "work" connotes something negative for some people and we want people to see these activities as positives. And, what is here is way more than The Feeling Alphabet as a stand-alone activity.

For us, the word "set" has meaning; a "set" suggests different items that work together with a shared set of ideas but not necessarily in the same order or the same way or with the same audiences in the same locations with each use. Sets are evidence of thematic links. The many activities and descriptions and examples comprising The Feeling Alphabet Activity Set share this theme: We are better off individually and collectively when we can name our feelings and understand our thoughts and behaviors. Everything within the Activity Set furthers this theme.

Think of this Activity Set like cooking utensils. A set of utensils is composed of a myriad of differently shaped items that share a common purpose: facilitating the making and serving of food. Calling something a "set" is a way, then, of underscoring similarities among different items. Within a set, items can be used at different times in different ways and among different groups; but the activities are held together with a deeply felt and important quest, in the case of "The Feeling Alphabet Activity Set" to name what we are feeling.

"The Feeling Alphabet Activity Set" has been prompted by the world in which we live in the US. Since the Covid-19 Pandemic along with racial tensions, food insecurity, wars and uncertainty, we recognize that if individuals at all ages and stages can identify **what** they are feeling, that very act of identification will help them and those around them navigate forward. Feelings matter, whether they're negative or positive. Naming our feelings is the first step in processing those feelings into thoughts and behaviors that are positive.

We want those using The Feeling Alphabet to know that we have both experienced across our lifetimes numerous negative and positive feelings. One of us has been subjected to anti-Semitism and sexual harassment. One of us has been called horrible names based on ethnic bias. We have memories of numerous events and interactions in which we were treated poorly and others in which we have been treated well. We have found joy and satisfaction in work and families. In short, we have a wealth of personal experience with feelings, thoughts and behaviors in addition to working with others with complex arrays of feelings culturally and linguistically. We live, learn and work in the world of feelings.

We also recognize that neither of us has personal experience of being black in the United States and, as such, we cannot speak for those who have and are suffering from the historical and ongoing trauma created by injustice, oppression and violence. What we do acknowledge, recognize and respect are the experiences of those who have incurred trauma and toxicity, all of which can impact the physical and mental health of all who are so affected.

Join us on a journey to name our feelings. If we do so, we will all be able to move forward more successfully – in school, in work, in our families, in our communities. We feel glad that you are engaging with us. Welcome to "The Feeling Alphabet Activity Set" and please share with us the effect and effectiveness of The Feeling Alphabet so it comes alive and can be published prospectively with your suggestions and examples.

# Why The Feeling Alphabet Activity Set Works So Effectively

# Why The Feeling Alphabet Activity Set Works So Effectively

## Our Powerful Emotions

Most children are perceptive about the world around them. They are hardwired with certain basic emotions: trust, love, happiness, surprise, anticipation, sadness, fear, anger, jealousy, shame and disgust. They have these emotions even before they have the words to express them. Emotions are how we experience and deal with situations that we find personally meaningful through "a complex reaction pattern, involving experiential, behavioral and physiological elements," as noted by the American Psychological Association.

## Our Stress and Emotions

Emotions and stress are intimately connected. Stress occurs when there is a mismatch between the perceived demands or threats being made on us and our perceived ability to cope with these demands or threats. To understand what is behind the stress and identify ways to de-stress, we need to identify more specifically the emotions that trigger the feelings of distress.

Consider this example of emotions and stress: Lucas' parents reported that their fourth-grade son refused to attend his online classroom when the switch from brick and mortar learning was made due to Covid-19. He had a big meltdown every morning before class was to begin. In the beginning, his parents were successful in persuading him to attend but his attendance diminished over time. They attributed their son's opposition as evidence of angry feelings Lucas had toward them and his teacher. But the real emotion behind the tension was their son's sadness about not being able to get individual, personalized attention from the teacher whom he really liked when he was in school. Forced attendance was not the pathway to helping Lucas deal with and handle his sadness due to loss of in-person attention; he wasn't mad at "learning;" he was mad at how he had to learn during Covid-19.

## Our Stress Busting Capacity

With few exceptions, we all have the capacity to regulate our stress. We survive and can even grow in positive ways during events that cause distress, trauma and uncertainty. However, that growth is not automatic because of the different ways in which trauma affects each of us. In the field of psychology, trauma refers to serious adversity, recognizing that the determination of what constitutes "serious adversity" differs from person to person. Trauma is, then, a "personal" experience, and it often occurs when the perceived demands on a person and that person's perceived ability to cope collide, as previously noted.

Children have the ability to self-regulate in a changing world filled with trauma. But, children can thrive when they receive support and guidance from their family and school community. Security, stability and safety matter. Some experts see younger children as poised to bounce forward better than adolescents following the Pandemic, protests against racism, social distancing and violence.

However, for very young children with severe and prolonged exposure to stress without protection and support ("toxic stress"), their experience impacts their developing brains, social and emotional development, learning, behavior regulation; the toxicity has a negative effect on their physical and mental health, all as noted by the Harvard Center on the Developing Child.

## The New Normal of Distress Tolerance

Words like "death," "infected," "quarantine," "social distancing," "tests," "deadly coronavirus," "outbreaks," "spikes," "killed in police custody," "I cannot breathe," "protest," "riots," "violence," "loss of jobs," "no money to buy food," flood the daily news, social media and daily conversations. These words and associated imagery of the impact of the Pandemic on physical and economic health, protests, social discourse and violence are stressful to all of us. Even if children do not understand these words, they can still be distressed by them. They exhibit feelings of fear, confusion, anger, and/or sadness during the continuous exposure and this can show up in demonstrations of cranky, agitated, worried behaviors. Like many of us, continued stress lowers our distress tolerance and in turn that tolerance continues to decrease as the stress persists over time.

## The Tuning Fork

Children of different ages experience the pandemic and social unrest very differently depending on how old they are, their physical location, the amount of attention they are paid by caregivers and other caring adults, and their understanding of the situations they and their caregivers are confronting. For many children, the just described words and imagery are traumatic; they hit a "tuning fork" in their brains and can also trigger memories of past feelings of a similar sort. Some children worry about their own health; many are concerned about the health of their parents, grandparents, teachers or friends. Fear of illness and death is plentiful. Some children are fearful that something bad will happen to their loved ones because of their skin color or their particular clothing choices or location in specific communities. Some are scared by the destruction of stores and fearful of walking by the streets and neighborhoods where the unrest occurs.

## Inherent Elasticity and Plasticity

We know that many children from stable, safe and secure families not only survive but continue to thrive during difficult times. They utilize their self-regulatory strategies that their families and schools taught them, and they engage reciprocally with adults who authentically care about them. They are "elastic" due to their nurturing and supportive environment that helps them with their concerns and feelings. They are able to bounce forward socially, emotionally and psychologically during this stressful time. Our brain's plasticity enables them to change and adapt.

## Absence of Elasticity and Plasticity

Children of families facing job losses, financial hardships, housing instability, food shortage, poor emotional support, fractured relationships or addictions due to or even before the Pandemic and the economic fallout are more likely to fare the worst. For families that already struggle with past trauma and ongoing toxic stress, their distress is further intensified with no end point in sight. Past trauma often triggers new trauma. The lack of stability, security and safety overloads these consequences on their body, mind, emotions and behavior.

## School Readiness Emotionally Speaking

How do children react and cope in times of distress and uncertainty? What emotions are they feeling, whether recognized or not? When physical attendance at school ceased in March 2020 in most locations and students had varying levels and quality of online learning in this gap period. We are still assessing how they developed after returning to school.

These are not easy things to track but we are trying. This past will inform our future.

The difficulty here is that the models for reopening were different and kept changing. There was unavoidable controversy as to which approaches were optimal for students and teachers and which were going to be sustainable without risk or with minimal risk. Some schools started online with teachers instructing from their actual classrooms. Other schools moved to differing hybrid models, with a certain number of days in person and other days online. In some schools, choice by students and their families as well as teachers was offered, meaning that some students learned online while others learned in person, all within the same classroom. Some online learning was synchronous; in other instances, it may have been asynchronous. And, there was the open question of when full-time, in-person learning in a brick and mortar school would return.

The point of these variations was that students of all ages and at all stages were making transitions and likely more than one transition over the academic year. One transition occurred, namely moving from in-person learning to some other approach, back in March of 2020. Upon returning in late summer/early fall 2020, schools were run differently; whatever model was used, there were added health protections when the learning was in person. Adjustment and readjustment become the watchwords for what students needed to navigate forward.

We can't ignore the feelings, thoughts, and accompanying behaviors that students experienced as they learned in whatever format it occurred. And, as added changes and adjustments were made, more feelings were evoked, including perhaps a dislike for the need for continuous disruption and readjustments. Equally important were the feelings, emotions, thoughts, and concerns of educators about themselves, the school where they were teaching in some format, and the students they were serving.

In sum, reopening schools was fraught with complexity in terms of more than physical distancing and health precautions; reopenings triggered the need to adapt to change.

# Not an Easy Set of Questions

Many students were excited to go back to school but had to adapt to all the new physical restrictions for in-school learning. They may have noticed students and teachers who were not returning for a wide-ranging group of reasons. Some children who felt anxious about social interaction were happy with remote learning, even if they were sad that they missed some in-school social activities. But this we know: we must avoid making assumptions about what children are feeling, including complex, contradictory, or overlapping feelings.

Instead, we need to ask broad questions that give children room to talk over what they're feeling. "How did you feel about what you saw on the news?" What did you make of what you heard?"  We need to help children to identify what they are feeling in a non-judgmental way and enable them to see that they can have more than a single feeling. If they do that, they can begin to recognize their positive and negative feelings. Highlighting their positive feelings reinforces their sense of well-being and naming the negatives helps them process of taming those negative feelings and emotions. We can help them to grow socially and emotionally during this new normal by naming the emotions that are there, but oft-times go unlabeled and undiscussed.

## Our Feelings are Expressions of our Emotions

With this Feeling Alphabet and the accompanying activity set, we seek to help students name their feelings. We believe that children can be helped if they are more in touch with the feelings they are experiencing after the Pandemic and with the racial tension and general unrest in our nation and the world. This process starts with finding pathways for identifying all of our feelings.

It is not easy to identify feelings for many children and adults; they may even be scared to say the words that come into their minds. We know that bottling up feelings does not erase them, and these feelings come out in other ways, often in ways that are not healthy for the individual experiencing them and can be discomforting or difficult for others around them. On the other hand, within some cultures, free expression of feelings is considered inappropriate; expression of feelings is measured and indirect. It is very important to respect culture and adapt the expression of feelings to the cultural, racial and ethnic norms.  Also selected words may be better at certain ages than others.

Consider these two examples. James, a high schooler, sits at home looking at the computer screen. He just stares at the blank screen. When his mother approaches him and asks what he is doing, he replies, "nothing."  When she asks him whether he wants dinner, he says, "whatever." Molly, usually an attentive child, is running around her house as if she had a case of the zoomies. She is jumping up on the sofa, she is pulling the dog's tail and when she sees her brother, she starts to run in circles around him, occasionally reaching out to touch his shirt. Both James and Molly have feelings that are manifested in behavior, but it is likely that these feelings have not been identified. Were they identified, adults could help both children understand and then process their respective behaviors.

Suppose one of James' parents gently said to him, "Is something bothering you? Is there anything I can do to help you feel better?" What if his father offered to play a video game with him, plunking himself down in front of the TV to show reciprocity and presence?

Now suppose that Molly's caregiver found a way to redirect her outsized behavior, rather than punishing her or telling her to stop. What if the caregiver said, "Wow, you have a lot of energy. How about we bake something you can deliver to the neighbors?" The idea is to refocus the energy productively and have the child focus on another person as a way of diffusing the self-focus of her activity. Developing empathy can help reroute emotions.

To return to James, what if his mother said to him, "Share with me whether you are sad. Do you miss your friends since school is closed?" With Molly, suppose her caregiver said, "Share with me what has you so excited? Do you miss running around the playground with your friends?"

If the parent/caregivers do nothing for James and Molly, consider what will occur when they arrive back at school. James will likely self-isolate, sit in the back row and not engage with his peers or his teachers; Molly will have trouble listening to instructions and sitting in one place and is likely to disrupt the class by teasing or bothering other students. Within a crowded school day, teachers may not have the opportunity to explore what is causing James and Molly's changed behaviors and may not see the behaviors as evidence of stress or trauma.

## We Can Improve Feeling Identification

The Feeling Alphabet and its activities are one approach for enabling children and adults to name positive and negative feelings. Look at this image of our brain and think about how it shows how feelings fill our heads – literally and figuratively. What's important to realize, too, is that feelings in the brain can affect our bodies and our actions. Stated another way, our brains have feelings and our bodies can act them out.

Here is a critical starting premise: People tend to ruminate on negative, as opposed to positive, feelings. That means negative feelings are a good pathway into expressing what is "on our minds." But, there need to be some positive feelings that counteract the negative ones, even if children and adult may want to focus on the negative feelings because they are easier to identify. If we don't allow the introduction of positive feelings – counterparts to the negative feelings -- our view of the world is dim indeed. We don't want children (or adults) to get stuck in the negative without seeing and feeling the positive.

Through dual feeling alphabets, with both positive and negative emotions being identified, we are enabling people – adults and children – to identify and process what they are feeling. Surely, as noted earlier, in the period after Covid-19 and racial tensions and economic uncertainty, we know a wide range of feelings abound.

Emotional
Brain

We have crafted, as an exemplar, a sample Feeling Alphabet for this unique period after COVID-19 and when racial and ethnic tensions cause global uncertainty. We identify but one set of words, leaving the door wide open for users of this tool to come up with their own feelings while seeing the feelings of others. Knowing that others can and do express positive and negative feelings for every letter of the alphabet is beneficial. Consider the pre-set alphabet as a permission-granting force.

Then, in addition to feeling identification, there are a set of activities that parents, caregivers and teachers can use to help students name and then tame their feelings. Importantly, the words we have chosen may differ from those of students (at whatever age and stage). Some of the activities may work more effectively with some students than others and that is why there are wide ranging choices for how we can get in touch with our feelings. For some, words are the pathway; for others, games are the way; for others, acting out and demonstrating feelings are the way.

How we get feelings identified matters way less than that we get children and adults to express feelings.

## The Cognitive Triangle

When we name our feelings, we begin to understand what we are sensing, experiencing and behaving. Often we see and judge a child's behavior based on what we see without paying attention to the underlying feelings and thoughts the child has related to the behaviors. Sometimes it is hard to see the connections between feelings, thoughts and behaviors before our eyes because all three can happen very quickly. It is easier to take behavior at face value and takes time to decode the feelings and thoughts and accompanying behaviors. On the other hand, we need to pay attention to all three interconnected triangles in order to manage them effectively.

Once The Feeling Alphabet has been created (which can be done over time – focusing just on certain letters at the start), an adult can ask the child who has filled in the words (or has the words dictated and filled in): "Share with me how that word (or those words) came to mind." We are exploring the thoughts behind the feelings.

## Decoding The Triangle

Decoding feelings, thoughts and behaviors is a skill that we learn. Our brain, an immensely complex organ, allows for different functions. Our brains have specific functions, and each part affects the other. We have the emotional brain, the thinking brain and the reptilian brain. Our Feeling Sleuth-Hound, on the next page, will demonstrate how this works as we sleuth out the feelings, thoughts and behaviors within our brains and bodies. Our goal is to help parents, teachers, and caregivers decode feelings, thoughts and behaviors so as to understand, connect and manage overwhelming negative emotions as well as positive ones.

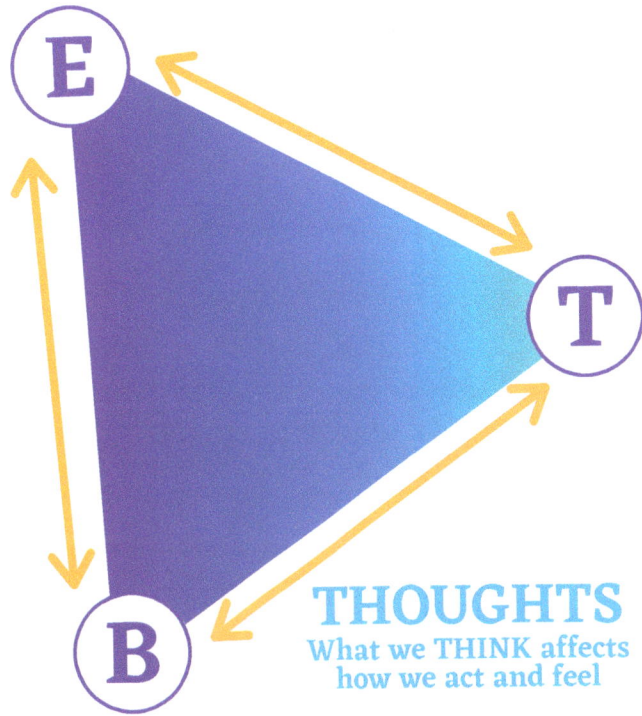

**EMOTIONS**
How we FEEL affects
what we think and do

**THOUGHTS**
What we THINK affects
how we act and feel

**BEHAVIORS**
What we DO affects
how we think and feel

# Meet the Feeling Sleuth-Hound

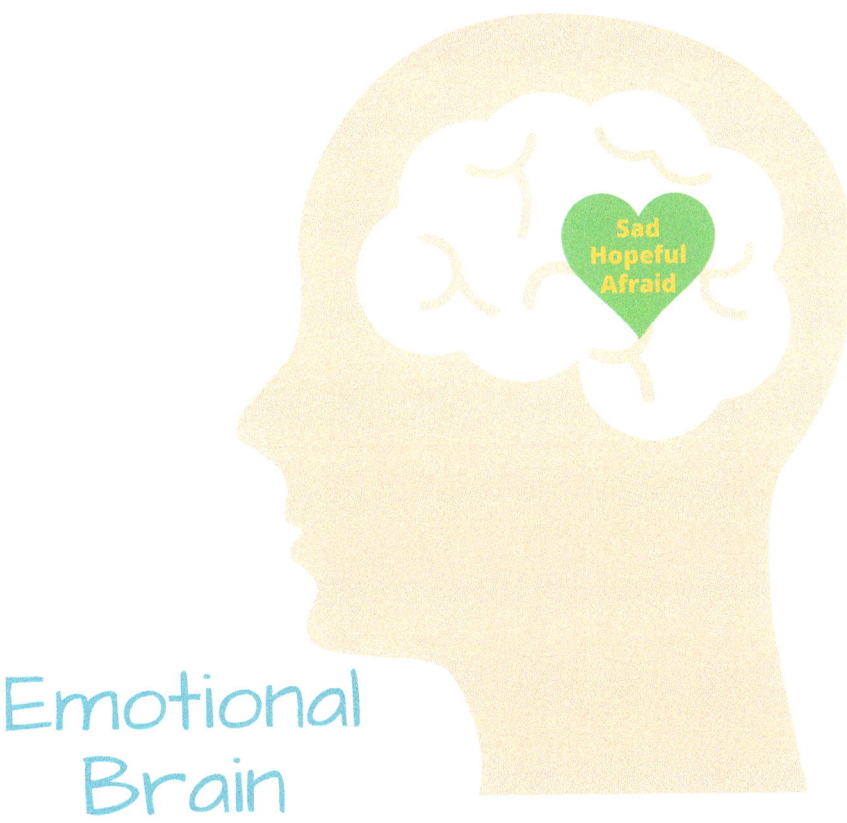

Sad
Hopeful
Afraid

# Emotional Brain

1) When you are looking for the feeling words that best describe how you feel, you are using your emotional brain. This is what naming negative and positive words of The Feeling Alphabet does at the initial stage.

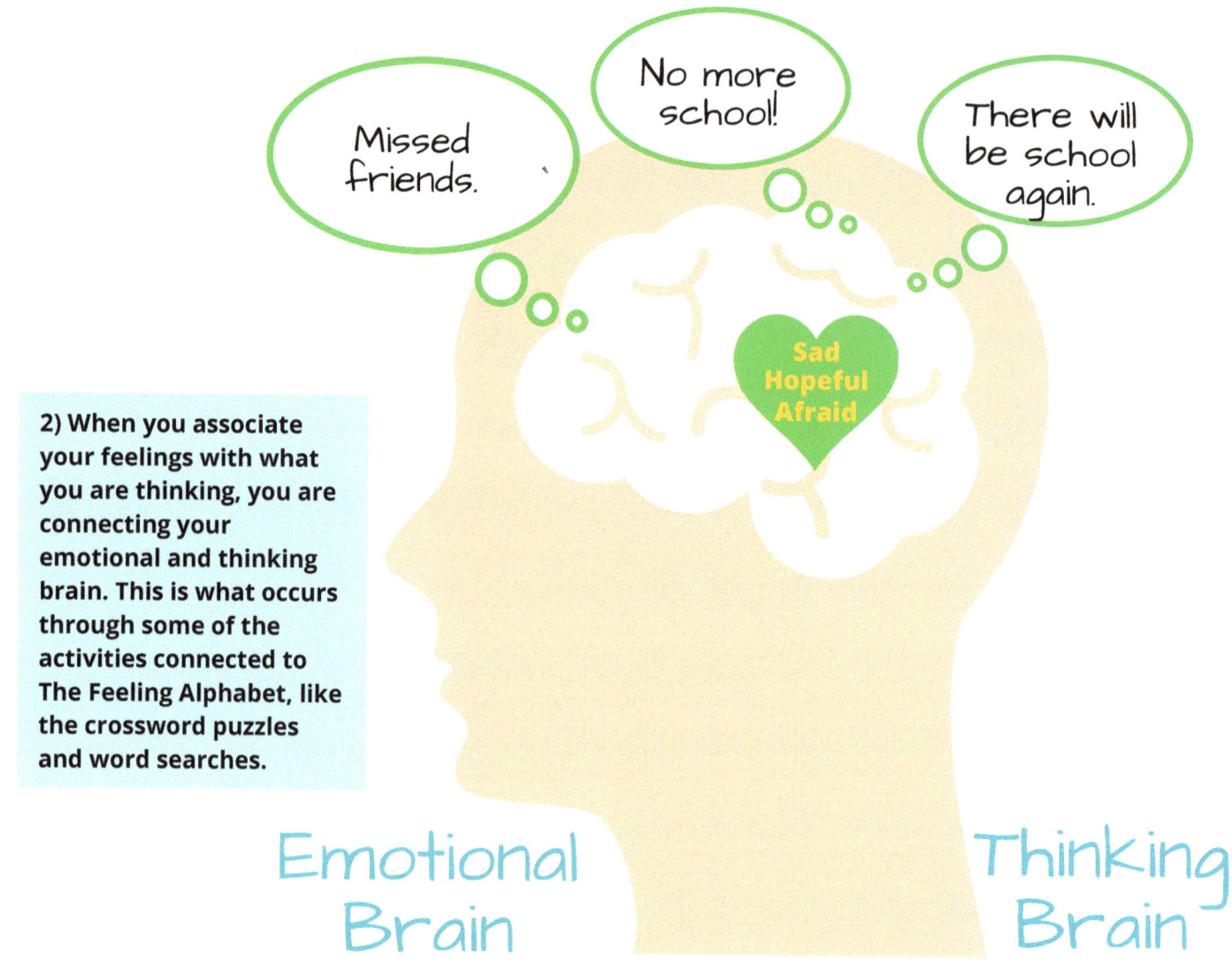

2) When you associate your feelings with what you are thinking, you are connecting your emotional and thinking brain. This is what occurs through some of the activities connected to The Feeling Alphabet, like the crossword puzzles and word searches.

3) When you connect your feelings, thoughts, body reactions and behavior, you are connecting your emotional and thinking brain. This means you are connecting to your feelings and acting on your thoughts through your behavior. You are demonstrating behavior that is caused by feelings and you are thinking about how to show those feelings so they can be identified.

**4) As a feeling sleuth-hound, you help your children/students/clients to decode feelings, thoughts and behaviors. You will help them by altering their thoughts and that in turn can change feelings and behaviors; feelings can change thoughts and behaviors too, and behaviors can change thoughts and feelings as well. The triangle runs in all directions. The Feeling Alphabet Activity Set works to activate this triangle.**

5) By paying attention to the here and now, we are less likely to get caught up with negative feelings and thoughts that are associated with the past and future and stop letting our mind take us wherever it wants to go.

We practice mindfulness. The Feeling Alphabet is a pathway toward this goal. Since it can be used in different ways at different times and used again and again in different order, we are able to open the door to feelings that children and adults are experiencing now.

## Mindful Caregiving Enables Mindful Children

When children learn to be mindful of their feelings, positives and negatives, we help them to reduce their distress especially when they are in a state of automatic, rapid and physiological arousal. When they are mindful of their overwhelming negative feelings we help them to redirect those feelings. This helps to slow down or even stop the big feelings from developing. It makes children/adults feel more in control, even if the feelings seem out of control. Regular practice of mindfulness, even when children are not in distress, improves learning, attention and concentration, creativity, problem solving and peer relationships with an overall sense of well-being.

Let's go back one more time and look at the behavior of Lucas, the 4th grader mentioned earlier. How did his parents find out his real feelings that were associated with not wanting to attend online classes? Rather than by forced online school attendance, which only irritated Lucas further, they decided to stop their behaviors because it was not working.

Suppose Lucas' parents had asked him the difference between in-person and online classes. Assume they were non-judgmental with respect to whatever thoughts and feelings he expressed and accepted what he said. When he said, "the class is boring," "it is stupid" and "a waste of time," they did not try to reason with him or change his mind. It is only after they got him talking that they realized that his anger and resentment were not at them or his teacher but the loss of the one-on-one attention that he was getting in person and not during the online group instruction. By acknowledging and labeling his feelings and thoughts of loss and grief due to school closure during the Pandemic, they would begin to come up with solutions. For example, they could reach out to his teacher and see if she was willing to provide him with some brief connection at the start and end of the school day and perhaps some personal attention with respect to his work. Once the teacher understands what was causing Lucas' absence and disinterest and she could find solutions to ameliorate his sense of alienation, it would be possible to restore his enthusiasm and improve his online attendance.

In short, identifying feelings is a pathway forward in these trying and uncertain times.

# The Intersectionality of Race, Ethnicity and Feelings

# The Intersectionality of Race, Ethnicity and Feelings

In the world filled with racial and ethnic tensions, it is important for these issues not to be swept under the proverbial rug or left to resolve themselves with the mere passage of time. Also, we know that these tensions create feelings in the persons who are being are treated "differently" because of being black or brown in a culture that can discriminate against those who do not look like them. These feelings are not just encountered by adults. Even if children are not familiar with the actual terminology surrounding racial and ethnic discrimination, there are keenly aware of their surroundings and can detect verbal and non-verbal cues of others.

These feelings about racial and ethnic tension, even though identifying them and expressing them to oneself and out loud may be difficult, do not go away or get processed by burying them. Instead, these feelings seep out, oft-times unknowingly and manifest themselves in thoughts and behaviors. Parents and teachers may not realize initially what is bothering their child or children; they may not have witnessed the behavior that was racially or ethnically triggering or even if they heard and saw it, they may not know how to respond to its occurrence.

The Feeling Alphabet and accompanying activities are one way of making what is covert overt.  The whole set of activities encourages the identification of feelings, both positive and negative. To concretize this effort and how it plays out in real life situations, we have crafted two scenarios. Both animate all the explanations and activities within this book. These examples, drawn from real life situations (altered to preserve privacy), allow readers to apply the principles of The Feeling Alphabet and feeling identification (naming) and the associated thoughts and behaviors.

Note the differences between the scenarios as you read. One involves a parent and child and a racist comment by a stranger in a public place. Not uncommon. The other scenario involves ethnic bias that occurs between students who know each other, and the results manifest themselves in the school environment. Not uncommon. Both scenarios focus on identification and processing of feelings and how to do that. Both recognize the legitimacy of feelings, despite their difficulty. Both scenarios explore what could happen were these feelings neither identified nor processed.

We hope these scenarios, and we are sure you can provide others, facilitate the discussion of feelings, thoughts and behavior in helping children, parents, teachers, and community organizations recognize and deal with racial and ethnic tension with the use of The Feeling Alphabet Activity Set.

## Keisha: Visible and Invisible Wounds of Racism

Children are easily upset by name calling. Prolonged and unresolved exposure to racist and ethnic slurs, prejudice and discrimination directly or indirectly have a detrimental effect on children's self-esteem, social identity and overall well-being. How do we help them to manage the visible and invisible wounds that came with overwhelming negative emotions?

Keisha Is a cheerful and easy going seven-year old girl. She was told to go back to Africa by a stranger while she was shopping with her mother, Rose, in a department store. Rose did not want to make a scene; so, she ignored the racial slurs and grabbed her daughter's arm and left the shopping aisle but stayed and finished shopping quickly.

Rose felt that the best way forward was to calm her own angry feelings toward what had happened before talking to Keisha. Her invisible wound of fear because of her skin color resurfaced because of the incident. She wanted her daughter to feel safe, secure and supported when they talked. Rose was honest with Keisha when they did talk. Rose told Keisha that she was shocked, fearful and threatened by what the lady said and might do. She said, "I felt scared and humiliated. I wanted to tell that lady what she said is wrong but decided not to do so because I don't know how this stranger would react; that's why I grabbed your hand and walked away."

Rose also made sure that she did not assume Keisha's experience and feelings are same as her own. She helped her to name her own feelings and the associated thoughts. She shared with her that "I felt better after we shared what happened in the department store." Rose also talked about her experience when she was a child hearing racial slurs and shared that, "I have seen some changes nowadays with some folks being more respectful toward black people. It will take time." Rose also told Keisha directly that racial slurs and being treated unfairly because of skin color is wrong. She plans to go to the store and report what happened to the management and she asked whether Keisha wanted to come along.

Racism and ethnic bias are topics about which conversations are hard because they trigger the invisible and visible trauma of one's experience and the feeling of being physically and psychologically unsafe. If we do not have the experience of being black or brown in the United States, we cannot speak in the same way to the racism and trauma that Rose and Keisha have suffered. Rose did all the right things to confront racism and discuss it with Keisha. She was mindful of her emotions and gave herself time to control them, asked questions rather than assuming Keisha's experiences were the same as hers and helped her to label and validate her feelings. Rose was honest and transparent with her own emotions and thoughts and called out that making assumptions and treating people by how they look is wrong. She modeled that she is not helpless by taking action and speaking to the manager, including with Keisha, a form of role-modeling action. Rose also shared a sense of hope and a right and safe way to speak out against racist behavior and ethnic bias.

## Rick: The Visible and Invisible Wounds of Ethnic Bias

Imagine that Rick was in 2nd grade. Both of his parents were American born. His grandparents on his mother's side were from the Philippines and his grandparents on his father's side were from Korea.

When the signs of the Pandemic appeared in China in early 2020, Rick's life changed almost immediately. Several of his closest friends refused to come to Rick's home for play dates and few children invited him into their home. At school, children refused to sit with him at lunch and several children whispered to each other, "there's the China virus kid" and "Rick is a virus" and "Rick will make you sick."

Rick did not share these occurrences with his family; he knew his parents kept their feelings to themselves. It was Rick's teacher who noticed that the usually engaged, popular student was sitting by himself, always diverting his eyes from others. He stopped playing in the playground during recess. He refused to read out loud. He ate lunch alone at the perimeter of the cafeteria.

Rick's teacher couldn't figure out what caused the sudden change because she did not have the time at that moment to examine his altered behavior. She just assumed Rick was moody or not feeling well. She didn't reach out to Rick's parents or the school nurse. She figured that time would be the cure. It wasn't and Rick remained out of sorts and disconnected from his friends until school was closed due to the Pandemic. One can only wonder how Rick will be when school reopens.

Suppose we change the scenario. What if the teacher had been able to pause, listen to the classroom chatter and rumors and then approached Rick when he was alone with this observation? "Rick, I've noticed you don't seem as happy as usual. Is there anything I can do to help you?" Suppose Rick didn't answer. Suppose the teacher then said, "Rick, why don't you read to me" and as they were reading together one of Rick's favorite stories, the teacher asked Rick if he was feeling differently due to the Pandemic.

Had the teacher used this different strategy, that would have created the opening Rick needed. Out came a flood of feelings and tears. Bottling up his feelings and not naming them allowed his isolation to continue. Sadly, we often miss what is right before us and small interventions, done sensitively, can have a profound positive effect.

## Next Steps

With these scenarios in mind, we can now turn to how to use The Feeling Alphabet and its accompanying activities with students and parents and teachers. We can consider this forthcoming section the one in which the rubber meets the road – the doing section – the section where we actually get our hands in the trenches and work through ways to discover our feelings and become more comfortable with them. This is hard. It is also, if done well, exciting and even fun at home, in school and in the community. The idea is not to judge or to criticize. It is the time to expand and in so doing to acquire a critical set of skills: the skills needed to discover, articulate and even act on our feelings, turning them into thoughts and actions.

# Suggestions for Activities Using The Feeling Alphabet

# Suggestions for Activities Using The Feeling Alphabet

**There is no one way to use The Feeling Alphabet and its activities. It can be done alone or in groups or in subgroups. It can be done in school, at home or in the community (whether online or in person). It can be done with adults and children of all ages and at all stages. Here are a set of suggestions and activities and approaches that can be used to animate further The Feeling Alphabet. We use the term "students" to refer to anyone using The Feeling Alphabet Activity Set, whether they are children, adults, clients, students, parents and/or teachers.**

- Students do not need to complete the whole alphabet at one time; instead, educators and students can work on select letters of the alphabet. They can proceed alphabetically (yes) or randomly, selecting letters that are particularly appealing. Letters can be revisited and feelings changed. Students can work alone or in groups or both.  If the process just involves word identification, it will not take lots of time and can be a quick class starting exercise.  With the added activities, it can be done in a break (online too) or as a separate activity for art or music or to regain class concentration.

- Students can pick the letters of their name or of the name of someone they care about when identifying accompanying positive and negative feelings. One could have students pick the name of the school they are attending.  So, for example, if they went to Adam School, they can start with the letters A, D and M.  And, they could have two positive and two negative words starting with A since Adam has 2 A's.

- Each page of alphabet letters has two images of the selected letter. One is already decorated with stars or colors or squiggles. Students can try to copy the image that appears or they can decorate the letters in a way of their own choosing. And, they can draw their own version of the letters (or trace them including unusual fonts).

- Students can play charades with their list of positive and words, acting out the selected feelings and seeing if others can guess what feeling is being expressed. This could be done with a single feeling or a chain of feelings.

- Students can draw their feelings once they have written their selected positive and negative alphabet words. That way, they are literally illustrating the alphabet.

- Students and teachers and families can create word puzzles and tongue twisters with positive and negative words. They can also use existing puzzles involving feelings that have already been created and they are available for individuals at differing age levels. There can be Feeling Word Searches, Feeling Crossword Puzzles, Feeling Scrambled Words. Below are some sites where existing and to be created puzzles appear, all without cost. We have included example Feeling Word Search and Feeling Crossword Puzzles so readers get a sense of the possible.

See our puzzle links on the next page.

**Links to puzzle and word search website where you can make feelings puzzles and crosswords**

https://www.teacherspayteachers.com/Product/Find-A-Feelings-Word-Search-Puzzle-979971?gclid=Cj0KCQjwy8f6BRC7ARIsAPIXQjj4gFAfdAEnzqhGW-ubLAU0fh1-aWsuiLKm4dC0dYJI7qfJhPFYyKMaAv_pEALw_wcB

https://mywordsearch.com/

https://www.freeprintablebehaviorcharts.com/

https://wordmint.com/public_puzzles/488464

http://puzzlemaker.discoveryeducation.com/

https://crosswordhobbyist.com/831488/Feelings-Up-and-Down

- Students can create puzzles for other students; simpler puzzles can be created for younger students; more complex puzzles for older students.

- Students can incorporate their positive and negative words into sentences or Mad Like Lib games where they fill in blanks in predetermined sentences. A sample set of Feeling "Mad Like Libs" is included and some tie into the above textual material, although they can be used independent of it.

- There are what we are calling brain bubbles (an image of our brain within our head!) at the end of this packet that students can use to express what is "in their heads;" the point is to show that we have feelings within us, even if we haven't yet expressed them. Also, we have stick figures with thought (word) bubbles emerging from them; these are opportunities for students and others to take the thoughts that are in their brains and move them out -- into sentences that can be said to others or at least said out loud. Taken together, they show the progression from having feelings in our mind and then expressing those feelings externally.

- Educators can, with students, create an installation art project with the letters and the accompanying positive and negative terms. This could be put in a prominent place in a classroom or in a hallway or even stairwell or displayed online and seen by viewers through a variety of approaches.

- It is worth using some form of technology once the full alphabets of all students are completed to determine what are the shared words among students for each letter (anonymous data collection). Online use of polls is one way of doing this as is clicker technology. In these ways, students know they are not alone in their feelings (and thoughts), something that is possible while preserving anonymity. For example, a poll could ask:  For a negative "A" word, 1. Angry 2. Absurd 3.  Argumentative 4.  Awful  5. Other (fill in).

- Consider activities that draw on the positive words (actually using them in the activity or in designing the activity). For example, for positive words starting with L, suppose a common word is laughter. Then, there could be an activity on jokes and riddles and writing them (which is always fun for students). Another activity is to create a positive word spinning wheel (like *Wheel of Fortune*) where a student spins and gets a word and then shares what that word means to him/her.

- Students can go out into nature and find items that evoke feelings (positive and negative) and draw or photograph the items and create an online alphabet that can be shared with others in the class.

- Students can create songs and dances related to the alphabet and/or the feelings generated by each word. Choreography is a skill and using letters and feelings as a theme has a richness to it. And, it allows students to express themselves without necessarily breaching personal privacy by saying what is on their mind in a vacuum. In the online world, students could share short videos or YouTubes of a song or dance that others could then learn and everyone could do it together.

- Consider the use of a visual or verbal "feeling thermometer." These can take a variety of forms, and they can be done using a numeric scale or with a color scheme (with red being hot and bothered and blue being calm and cool with other colors in-between). They can be personalized and contextualized.

Here are some links to sample feeling thermometers. Note the differences among them. https://www.teacherspayteachers.com/Product/Feelings-Thermometer-and-Cards-2820015?gclid=EAIaIQobChMI8cLXvZ-q6wIVg4nICh1HsAMvEAQYAyABEgLPmPD_BwE;  https://lighthouse-press-inc.myshopify.com/products/feeling-thermometers-small

We have included a blank feeling thermometer which can be completed and changed and added to with creativity and adjusted for the age and stage of the students using it.

The thermometers can be used in different ways and to express different ranges of feelings -- good to bad, hard to easy, miserable to happy, boring to excited to learn online or at school. On a numeric thermometer, be sure to give concrete examples of the two opposite anchors and incremental steps in-between. The scale moves up or down in increments of a person's choosing. In a given day, a student could be in different spots on the thermometer and so have students and teachers complete together the thermometer several times a day.  That can help them to identify how they are doing. The key is to recognize that feelings are not static and something can be done to address them.

It's important to make sure that anonymity is preserved if desired. This can be done in a myriad of ways in both the in person and online environment. By way of example, using stickies in person or a poll on line would achieve these ends.

- There can be blank illustrations of the emotional brain and thinking brain. These could then be colored in based on students' feelings or thoughts of the beginning, middle and the end of the school day. Students can also write to express how they feel, what they think and say. They can also draw their behavior next to an image. This is a variant of the feeling brain image and the stick figure with the thought bubble.

- Students can play and imagine the role of the Feeling Sleuth-Hound or any of their favorite animals or characters individually or as a group to explore the connection of feelings and thoughts and behaviors of a character based on a made-up story.

- Mindfulness can be introduced using the power of imagination and play. For example, one could say, "Pretend you are the Feeling Sleuth-Hound. How do you go about solving a mystery or dealing with a troubling situation? How would you regulate your thoughts and feelings when you are in a dangerous situation?"

- Catch phrases of the Feeling Sleuth-Hound include: "Feelings come and go;" "Watch our thoughts and not be our thoughts;" "Managing stress by getting ahead of stress;" "Mindful teachers lead to mindful students;" "Mindful parents lead to mindful children;" and "Try not to take things too personally even if they feel personal." These thoughts and phrases can be part of a sing or dance along or a rap piece or slam poetry or spoken word events.

- Consider strategies that the Feeling Sleuth-Hound uses when it feels stressed and sees a STOP sign. Here is a decoding of a STOP sign: S stands for stop, T stands for take a deep breath, O stands for observe, P stands for proceed. Another way to do this is to have the Sleuth-Hound find the letters S, T, O and P and create a sign with them (piece them together like a collage) and then identifying the actions that each letter represents.

- Create your own snow globes as a project with synthetic snowflakes and add a key calming object inside. These can be used repeatedly when feelings seem too intense. Just shaking and watchful waiting until all the snow settles is beneficial. We can add a breath-in and breath-out exercise while watching the snow globe, another mindfulness exercise. There are pre-made "snow globes" that can be purchased where one can insert a larger object to symbolize calm and positive feelings when the snow is settling to the bottom. For an example, see: https://amzn.to/2YE0TDB

- In a time of social distancing where hugs and handshakes and other forms of physical engagement are limited, we can still create emotional engagement with others. Ponder several ways to do that are safe and powerful connectors. For example, consider linking people together with each holding a knotted portion of a beautifully decorated rope or long band. One can create one of rubber bands or even ribbons. Remember the old game of telephone? Take two cans, connect them with a cord that is 10 feet long or more and talk to someone else. Use the outdoors where distancing is easier. Create an art arrangement of colorful pillows or mats that are each 10 feet apart. Place them in different designs. Photograph them with and without people on them. Pair the pictures to show: connection and connecting space.

- Culture matters. We need to pay attention to how feelings, thoughts and behaviors manifest differently because of cultural differences and modify our approaches to be culturally respectful and relevant. We should pay attention to what feeling words people use and how they express themselves verbally and non-verbally. We must value how they explain their associated thoughts and feelings. Together, we can strategize a culturally sensitive and relevant approach to solve a problem.

- For young children, drawing, painting or acting out stories with toys can be helpful tools for expressing thoughts and feelings that aren't easy to put into words. Let children do it themselves. Offer choices when needed. Do consider not only the age but the emotional level of the child in designing activities.

- While the selection of words in not an activity involving judgment as to the nature of the selected words, educators need to be on alert if a student's choice of negative words suggests self-harm or harm to others or some deeper feelings that seem out of the norm. Consider reaching out to a mental health professional to get advice as to whether this student needs some professional intervention.

## CONCLUSION

Be creative and inventive. Share your ideas with us. We plan to create a virtual forum to learn about your work. We consider the Feeling Alphabet to be an iterative project. We can and will add in your examples, your images, your suggestions, your words. So, be a part of "The Feeling Alphabet Activity Set." And, be assured that you are not alone and if you can share your feelings, you are already feeling better!

The Feeling
Alphabet

A to Z

Angry

Awesome

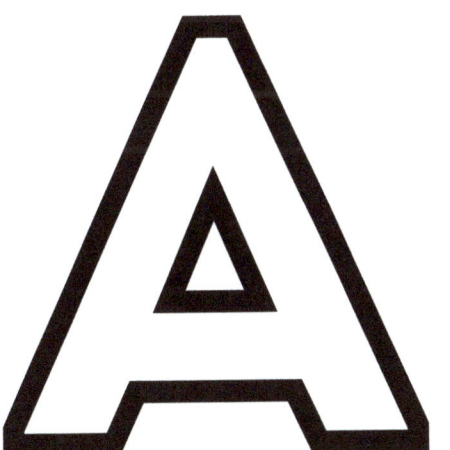

Bored

Better

_____                    _____

Confused  Creative

**Depressed**  **Delighted**

_____     _____

Enraged

Empathy

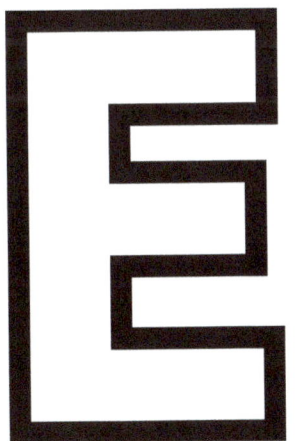

Furious                                        Friendly

_____                                    _____

Grief

Grateful

_____          _____

Hurt 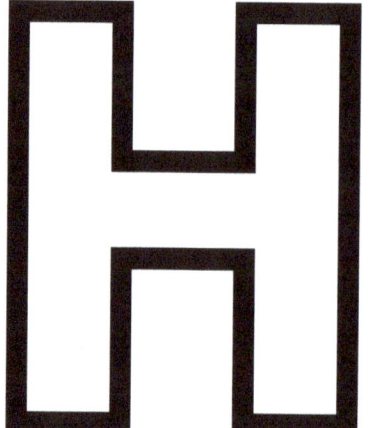 Happy

_____ _____

Isolated  Included

Jittery

Joyful

Kooky

Kind

Lonely  Likeable

———————                      ———————

Misunderstood                    Mighty

Nauseous  Nourished

_____  _____

Overwhelmed

Optimistic

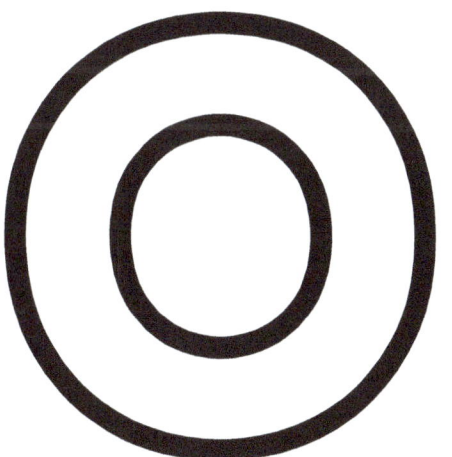

Panicky

Popular

_____    _____

P

Queasy  Quiet

_____ _____

Resentful  Respected

_____                _____

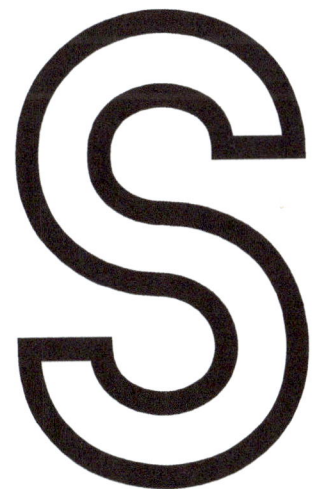

Scared

Smart

_____

_____

Tense

Terrific

Uncomfortable

Understood

_____

_____

Victimized                          Valued

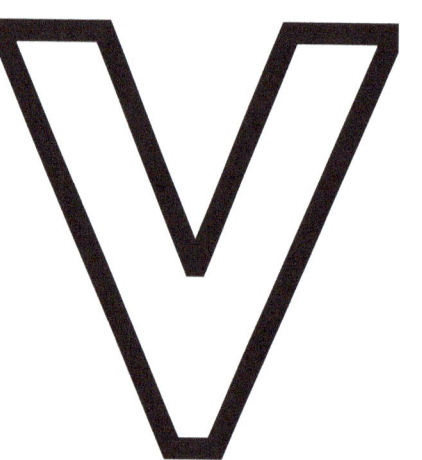

_____               _____

Worried 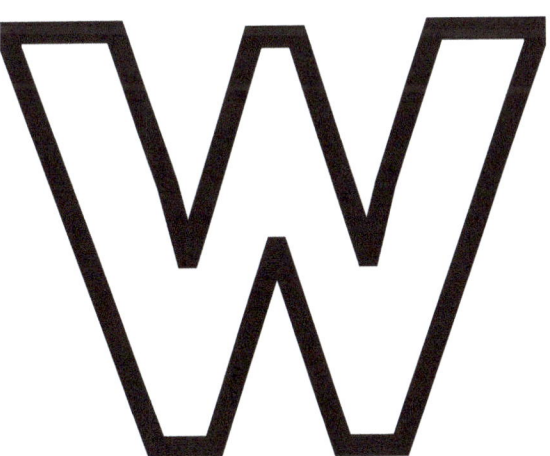 Wonderful

_____                              _____

X-Rayed        Xenial

_____        _____

Yucky

Yummy

——————

**Y**

Zoned Out

**Z**

Zippy

**Z**

_____     _____

# Feelings
# Activities

# Feelings Word Search

```
E G H X P L E A S E D Y R B U I I I W O
B W O Z J H G R G T V E O V Y P K E N W
D G N S A X R F Q U I L F P P Q D G Z E
V Q K Z F S I J D W G C E Q S E D C P G
B R T N T K A D Z D O E G E N H E R F L
H F D E U L A V L N L N C A U A T A W D
B E L I E V E D F S I U E R N Z A N D J
P A S G Y W K U A T R M T N K E M K E J
E K H M R M S P S E E R O I Y M I Y G E
I V S F A E C U D D D Y D M T B N W V N
F W J V D D R Z P U E E F N E A A E K I
T E N S E T L T A D O M I E Z D F F R Y
A Y H A P P Y Z X D E R W F A A F A S K
N U X S R T G V E W Q N P N S R N A A R
L I K E D M A V B T H Z N G F I F N D E
Y T S E T A E D U N I Z X W K L T U U P
F V N W N E Z A X R Z D E V I T C A L S
L F L G P Y D E R O N O H R O J M D S X
G I R I O T I R E D S D E R A C S F J I
H Y A L T M H H D E V O L Z T L C K U S
```

active
angry
animated
annoyed
bad
believed
confused
cranky
demeaned
fearful
happy
honored
hurt
liked
loved
mad

peeved
perky
pleased
proud
sad
safe
satisfied
scared
secure
sleepy
tense
testy
tired
trusting
valued

# Feelings Word Search
## Answer Key

```
E G H X P L E A S E D Y R B U I I I W O
B W O Z J H G R G T V E O V Y P K E N W
D G N S A X R F Q U I L F P P Q D G Z E
V Q K Z F S I J D W G C E Q S E D C P G
B R T N T K A D Z D O E G E N H E R A L
H F D E U L A V L N L N C A U A T N W D
B E L I E V E D F S I U E R N Z A N D J
P A S G Y W K U A T R M T N K E M I E J
E K H M R M S P S E E R O I Y M I Y N I
I V S F A E C U D D D Y D M T B N W V N
F W J V D D R Z P U E E F N E A A E K I
T E N S E T L T A D O M I E Z D F R Y K
A Y H A P P Y Z X D E R W F A A F A S E
N U X S R T G V E W Q N P N S R N A D R
L I K E D M A V B T H Z N G I F N D U P
Y T S E T A E D U N I Z X W K L T U U P
F V N W N E Z A X R Z D E V I T C A L S
L F L G P Y D E R O N O H R O J M D S X
G I R I O T I R E D S D E R A C S F J I
H Y A L T M H H D E V O L Z T L C K U S
```

# Crossword Feelings Up and Down

## WORD LIST

ANGRY      SAFE
CONFUSED      SECURE
HAPPY      TENSE
HONORED      TIRED
PERKY      VALUED
SAD      WORRIED

## Across

1 What you feel when you are filled with joy (starts with H)
4 What you feel when you are mad (starts with A)
6 What you feel when things are not clear (starts with C)
7 What you feel when people respect you and your work (starts with H)
10 What you feel when you are safe (stars with S)
11 What you feel when you are not happy (ends with D)
12 What you feel when you are not fearful (ends with E)

## Down

2 What you feel when you are active and awake (starts with P)
3 What you feel when people care about you (starts with V)
5 What you feel when you are concerned (starts with W)
8 What you feel if you have not had enough sleep (ends with D)
9 What you feel when you are not relaxed (ends with E)

# Crossword
## Feelings Up and Down
### Answer Key

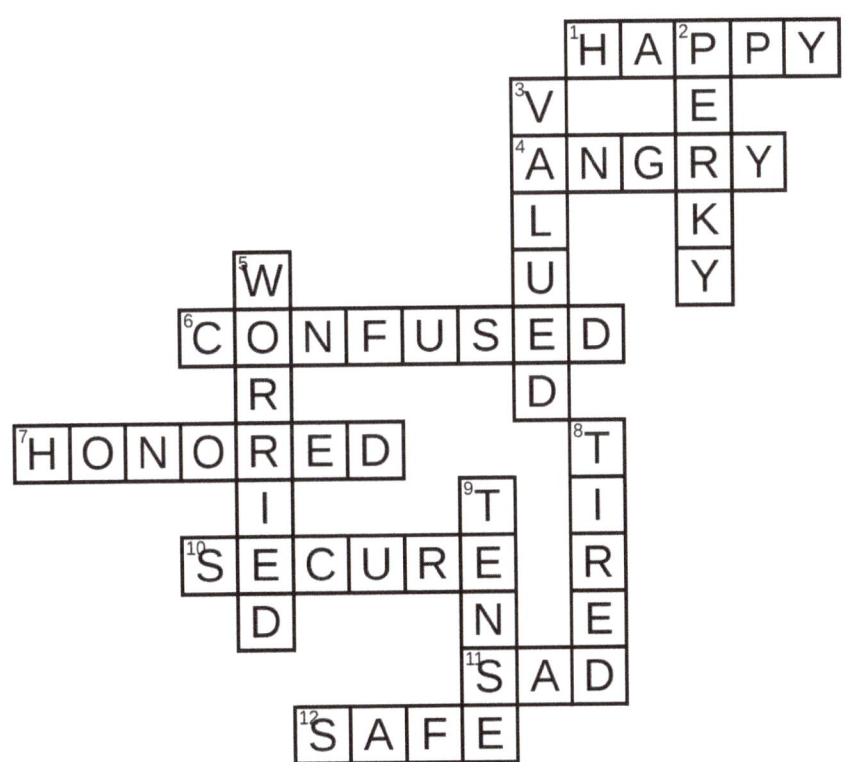

# Feelings Thermometer

# Feeling "Mad-Like Libs"

Lissa, I am feeling so _____ I could run around the block twenty times in my bathing suit.

Lance, I am very _____ and want to tell that teacher how wrong he is.

Sandi and Jacob both reported that they felt _____ when they saw the amazing sail boat passing by them.

Robert and Rachel are _____; their grades on that difficult test was not as bad as they expected.

Social distancing makes me _____; it is a way of separating people who want to be more connected.

Masks are required in many situations; that makes me feel _____ and _____.

Our world is filled with uncertainty and confusion and difficulty; that makes me _____.

I feel so _____ I want to throw a ball through a window but I won't.

# Feeling "Mad-Like Libs"

I wish I didn't feel so _____; then I'd be calmer and happier.

My best friend is amazing; when I am with my best friend, I feel _____.

Fredda teases everyone who is not like her; this makes me so _____.

I understand that recognizing what one is feeling matters; often, I can't recognize when I am _____.

Rose thought she had control of the situation; she felt _____ and when she thought she had no control she felt_____.

Lucas thought virtual learning was _____ when he thought he wasn't getting the personal attention from his teacher.

When I take things too personally, I feel _____ and when I take things less personally, I feel _____.

When I thought someone treated me unfairly because of my skin color, I felt _____.

# Feeling "Mad-Like Libs"

When I thought someone was respectful and curious about who I am, I felt_____.

When I am stressed, I feel _____ but after I take several deep breaths and practice self-reflection, I feel _____.

When I am shaking and looking at the flying snow-flakes in the snow globe, I feel _____, and when the last flake settles to the bottom, I feel _____.

Keisha feels _____ when her friends get picked on by others.

When someone calls me names, I feel _____.

John will feel _____ if he goes back to school and see his friends again but he will feel_____ if he cannot and has to learn from home.

# My Feelings, Thoughts and Behaviors

# Stick Figure-it-out

# Trauma Resources

***Trauma Doesn't Stop at the School Door: Strategies and Solutions for Educators, PreK—College***
By Karen Gross (Teachers College Press, June 2020) - available on Amazon.com

***Mending Education: Finding Hope, Creativity and Mental Wellness in Times of Trauma*** By Karen Gross and Edward K.S. Wang (Teachers College Press, September 2024) - available on Amazon.com

## YouTubes on Social Distancing prepared by Karen Gross

https://www.youtube.com/watch?v=fdwaUCEbhBk  (without music)

https://www.youtube.com/watch?v=Me5YVuCtrqk (with music)

## YouTubes on Social Distancing prepared by Drs. Wang and McLean

**Key-Key the Monkey and the Coronavirus Intruder** (English narration)
https://www.youtube.com/watch?v=n7fXbMhKPZI&t=151s

**Resilience assessment tool**
https://www.youtube.com/watch?v=EtND8CDacDU

**Cultural competence seminars**
https://www.youtube.com/watch?v=YBpXuyWXq8E

# About the Authors

**Ed K.S. Wang, M.S., Psy.D.**

Edward K. Wang, a grandparent and psychologist, promotes the social and emotional well-being of children across the globe. As the Director of Policy and Planning for the Division of Global Psychiatry, Massachusetts General Hospital, a former member of the National Advisory Council, Department of Health and Human Services and a public steward of the Massachusetts Department of Mental Health, he continues to call attention to the resiliency and hope, growth and healing of mental ill adults and children. Ed is the co-author along with Karen Gross of the book "Mending Education: Finding Hope, Creativity, and Mental Wellness in Times of Trauma."

Ed K.S. Wang, M.S., Psy.D.
Director of Policy and Planning
Chester M. Pierce MD Division of Global Psychiatry
Massachusetts General Hospital
Assistant Clinical Professor of Psychology, Part-Time
Harvard Medical School
617-872-4234, ekwang@mgh.harvard.edu; ed.global.diversity@gmail.com
http://www.mghglobalpsychiatry.org/staffpages/edwardwang.php
http://http://www.mghglobalpsychiatry.org/

**Karen Gross**

Karen Gross is an author and educator who specializes in trauma and student success academically and psychosocially. In addition to her writing and speaking engagements, she teaches students of all ages and at all stages from PreK through graduate school. Karen is the co-author along with Ed K.S. Wang of the book "Mending Education: Finding Hope, Creativity, and Mental Wellness in Times of Trauma." In addition, she is the author of more than nine children's books (in addition to her adult books), all of which are trauma responsive. She is the pet parent of the Feeling Sleuth-Hound.

karengrosscooper@gmail.com
www.KarenGrossEducation.com

# About This Book

The Feeling Alphabet Activity Set is a resource to help students, families, teachers, and community members identify their feelings, including those generated by COVID-19 and recent racial tensions.

The premise of The Feeling Alphabet Activity Set, co-authored by Dr. Ed Wang and Karen Gross, is that it is critically important to be able to name one's feelings (negative and positive ones alike). If you cannot name feelings, then you cannot tame them.

People of all ages and stages can use this activity set; the activities can be ramped up and down. And, they are fun and engaging. It is NOT a work book -- with the emphasis on work.

Instead, it is about finding a pathway into one's feelings.

It is our hope that when you use The Feeling Alphabet Activity Set you will share the results with us, including additional exercises, drawings and new images.

For additional information, please contact
Karen Gross at karen.cooper.gross@gmail.com.
Also visit the author's website below:

https://karengrosseducation.com